MICHELLE OBAMA BOOK

The Biography of Michelle Obama

University Press

INTRODUCTION

Observers note that there are two kinds of first ladies: (1) those who slip into the background shadows, and (2) those who stand out as leaders in their own right. Those in the former camp remain almost invisible while their husbands enjoy and endure the heat of the limelight. These first ladies may occasionally be spotted with the President during important events, but they will rarely speak publicly about issues that matter to them. As a result, they are seldom remembered except as footnotes in history books. Those in the latter group stand out as community and cultural leaders, speaking out on issues that are both important to them and harmonious with the initiatives of their husband's administrations. As a result, they become role models for the people of the United States and the world - and especially for the millions of women and girls who look up to them.

There are two kinds of people in the world: (1)

those who passively accept the hand they were dealt, content to stay in their lane, and (2) those who pursue more, pushing the boundaries to change the world in some way.

Michelle Obama, the wife of Barack Obama and First Lady of the United States from 2009 to 2017, has shown through her words and actions that she is the strong leader kind of First Lady and the quintessential boundary-pushing, world-changing kind of person. As a young girl, she pushed beyond the comfort of home. She pushed beyond being the woman her teachers and counselors decided she would be. She aimed higher. She broke the mold. She went to Princeton. She graduated from Harvard Law. As a lawyer and community leader in Chicago, she worked hard to accomplish more than just a paycheck. She reached out to the community, worked closely with the poor, and labored to effect positive change in her city. As a wife and mother, she was determined to be there for her two daughters while also continuing to support the community in powerful ways. Finally, as a wife, she supported her husband in the race for President, eventually taking America's culture by storm and becoming a role model for women and girls all over the world.

Michelle's legacy - still going strong as she continues to grow and lead - is one of determination, courage, and leadership. This book, though, looks deeper than the public face that has graced the covers of countless newspapers and magazines. This book looks at the woman behind the fame - the scholar, lawyer, mother, wife, advocate, and icon. This book is about a little girl who helped care for a sickly father, attended church every Sunday, and worked hard to excel in school. This book is about a heritage as storied, diverse, and multicultural as America's own history.

Michelle Obama's story begins with Michelle Robinson's story, the girl who grew up in south Chicago and excelled in many ways long before she met Mr. Obama and was set on the path to becoming the First Lady. And, in fact, before we can talk about Michelle Robinson, we have to look at her family and heritage, at treasures that had been hidden from even her until after she'd already moved into the White House.

Michelle Obama In A Nutshell

In Chapter 1, we'll look at the Robinson and Shields families, at the family lines that led to Michelle Robinson. We'll see how her story goes back to slaves, immigrants, and rich slave owners, meaning her bloodline embodies the very diversity we see in America today. Then, in Chapter 2, we'll take a peek at Michelle Robinson's early childhood. What schools did she learn at? What was her family life like? And what challenges did she face from an early age?

In the following chapter, we'll see how a young woman found maturity and independence in college. We'll also see how trials, revelations, and doubts struck at the very core of who she was. Her aspirations clashed with her heritage. Her future seemed at war with her past, and those doubts had to be settled before she could truly succeed.

In Chapter 4, Michell Robinson becomes Michelle Obama as she and Barack meet, fall in love, and face tragedy together. In the chapter that follows, more hardship and tragedy grip the young family as they seek to have children. At the same time, her career develops, allowing her to create the changes she desires most in the communities she cares about.

Next, we'll see how this growing family faces new challenges as Barack seeks greater positions in public service, eventually becoming a US senator. Through this time, Michelle struggles to balance motherhood, her own career, and supporting her husband in campaigns and the trials of leadership.

In Chapter 6, we see Michelle supporting her family through the trials of a presidential campaign, one that Barack won in 2008. In the following chapters, we see how Michelle learns what it means to be First Lady and how she grows in popularity, becoming a role model for young women across the globe. We'll also see how she embraces initiatives that she cares about, such as "Let's Move!" and "Let the Girls Learn."

Finally, in Chapter 9, we'll see how Michelle continues to lead and create change after leaving the White House through speaking events, books, TV, and podcasts.

Themes From Michelle's Life And Career

As we look at Michelle's life, from childhood through school and family and the White House and beyond, we'll see common themes play out over and over.

One theme is the concept of "becoming." Young Michelle Robinson took on challenges that led to her having to adapt and grow into new roles. It's no coincidence that Michelle's own 2018 memoir was titled *Becoming*.

Another theme we'll see is that of balance. When one is passionate about two different things, like being a good mother and supporting a husband's political ambitions, one can easily feel pulled in diametrically opposed directions. But learning to balance those things is essential to success (and staying sane).

Another key theme in Michelle's life has been education, which is why education became a passion she speaks about as much as she can after leaving the White House.

Finally, one last theme we'll see throughout her life is self-knowledge. Michelle has to be secure in who she is in order to overcome challenges and not get lost in the winds of others' expectations.

As these themes play out, we'll see how Michelle Obama has proven to be a driven, courageous, and hopeful leader.

To start with, let's look into Michelle's past, to the family roots that shaped her from an early age.

CHAPTER 1

Multicultural Ancestry

G rowing up in South Chicago, Michelle Robinson didn't know much about her family history. Beyond parents and grandparents, how many of us know much at all about the generations that come before? Michelle knew that her ancestry was varied and that she even had white ancestors at some point, but she didn't know much more than that.

Her family, on both her parents' sides, had moved north during a period often called the "Great Migration" of the twentieth century, a time when many freed black slaves or their children moved north to urban areas to find work in factories, seeking to leave behind the poverty and memories of slavery that drenched the southern rural lives they led.

Of course, becoming globally famous has its

benefits. In Michelle's case, it was only after her husband was elected president that historians and genealogists took an interest in her heritage. New connections were made, and a grand mystery was opened, details unfurling like the petals of a blossoming flower. Michelle would go on to meet living relatives she'd never known she had. As her family tree was clarified—and even detailed in books such as *American Tapestry: The Story of the Black, White, and Multicultural Ancestors of Michelle Obama* by Rachel L. Swarns—it became clear that all four of Michelle's grandparents had a diverse ancestry, creating a vast heritage that included Irish, English, and Native American roots.

Let's pull a few threads of that tapestry and see what stories surface, starting with Michelle's mother's side of the family.

Michelle's Mother's Family Line: The Shields'

Michelle's mother's name is Marian Shields Robinson, and, as of the time of this book's publication, she is still alive. Marian was a full-time stay-at-home mom while Michelle and her brother, Craig, were young. When Michelle started high school, Marian got a job as a secretary at Spiegel's catalog store. Later, when the Obamas moved to the White House, Marian moved in with them to help raise Michelle's two daughters.

The Shields family line is fascinating, leading back to Michelle's white ancestor, most likely a young man named Charles.

The book *American Tapestry* opens with a description of a young woman named Melvina Dosey Shields. Melvina was born as a slave in South Carolina, and she was sold to a man named Henry Walls Shields, who owned a large farm in Clayton County, Georgia. Melvina was a girl when the change in owners meant she moved from South Carolina to Georgia and into the Shields' home.

Very little is known about this young Melvina, but we do know that she was freed after the American Civil War. At that time, she already had children, including a boy she named Adolphus T. Shields, who was half white.

Now free, Melvina stayed near the farm she'd been a slave in. She had several more children, many of whom were obviously half white, yet she never revealed who their father was. Historians used contextual evidence and DNA testing to try and figure out who Adolphus's father could have been, and every line of evidence points to Henry Walls Shields' son, Charles Marion Shields.

Questions about Melvina's life as a slave are disturbing and hard to answer. Was she raped in that house by the master's son? Were they secretly in love? It seems that Melvina was not resentful of the children she bore since she chose to stay around after gaining freedom and because she kept the Shields name for herself (until, years later, she married another man) and for Adolphus.

Either way, it is certain that Adolphus grew up and married, eventually moving to Birmingham, Alabama. He would become Michelle's great-great-grandfather.

The Robinsons: Michelle's Fathers' Side

Michelle's father was Fraser Robinson III, and he worked for the water plant of the city of Chicago. Although he dealt with MS, a chronic and debilitating illness, he also served as a Democratic precinct captain, which is an elected position. A precinct captain is responsible for facilitating voter registration in the local area. He also facilitates absentee ballot access, distributes pamphlets and campaign propaganda for the local and national democratic candidates, and does whatever he can to support party campaigns in his community. All of this is a lot of work, and precinct captains usually don't get paid for their work, although some local communities provide a small stipend.

Fraser Robinson III died in 1991, finally succumbing to his illness. His life and death left a great impact on Michelle's life. But the Robinson family line also left a larger cultural impact on her.

The Robinsons go back to the Gullah people of South Carolina's "Low Country." The so-called low country stretches along the coast from Cape Fear, North Carolina, all the way down to Jacksonville, Florida. In this somewhat isolated region, the Gullah people lived as freed slaves that carved out a life for their families in rural communities. Because they were so isolated for generations, their culture and language were largely preserved for a long time. In fact, while it can be argued that African American influences have shifted the culture of the United States from the days of slavery down to now, it can also be said that the pure culture of the Gullah people has been a powerful influence on modern African American culture. This makes the low country the driving engine of much of the language, music, and food that Southern and American cultures are known for.

Jim Robinson, Michelle's great-great-grandfather, was born a slave in 1850 at Friendfield Plantation, which was located near Georgetown, South Carolina. At the age of 15, he was given his freedom, and—like Melvina Shields—he chose to stay in the area.

Much of Michelle's family on her father's side still live in the Georgetown area. Her grandfather, Jim Robinson Jr., moved back to South Carolina after retiring in Chicago.

It was in Chicago that Fraser Robinson and Marian Shields met and married, eventually giving birth to two beautiful and bright children: Craig and Michelle Robinson. In the following chapter, we'll look at Michelle's life growing up in south Chicago.

CHAPTER 2

Early Life

M ichelle LaVaughn Robinson was born on January 17, 1964, on the south side of Chicago, as American Tapestry puts it, "in a working-class corner of the city's storied black community, just like her parents." Both Fraser Robinson and Marian Shields Robinson were life-long Chicagoans, and their two children would grow up in much the same culture they had, only a bit more modern.

Growing Up In A "Conventional" Family Home

Michelle grew up at 7436 South Euclid Avenue in a two-story house owned by her great aunt. The aunt lived on the ground floor, while the Robinsons lived upstairs.

It wasn't just Michelle and her parents, of course. Her brother, Craig, was less than a year older than she was. He could continue to play an important role in Michelle's life, as we'll see later in this book.

Michelle described her childhood as a "conventional" one. For example, she recalls the family playing monopoly together in the evenings and on rainy days. "When I was a kid," she writes in her memoirs, "my aspirations were simple. I wanted a dog. I wanted an hour that had stairs in it—two floors for one family. I wanted, for some reason, a four-door station wagon instead of the two-door Buick that was my father's pride and joy." Sounds much like a conventional childhood, doesn't it?

One aspect of Michelle's childhood wasn't quite conventional: her father's health. As mentioned, Fraser Robinson III suffered from multiple sclerosis, a chronic and debilitating disease that would eventually take his life in 1991.

And yet, at this point, early in Michelle's life, the MS wasn't much of an issue. Her family attended church services at the South Shor United Methodist Church, and Michelle's family was large, loud, and happy. She often saw her extended family on both her parents' sides.

Her happy childhood spilled out from her second-story home and into elementary school, where a key aspect of Michelle's life comes into play.

Elementary School Years

Michelle and Craig attended elementary school just down the street from their house, meaning they could walk there most days. It was while at school that Michelle first fell in love with learning. Education, a central theme of her life many years later, was a love that grew from seeds planted as early as elementary school, seeds that would grow into a tree-like passion that formed her personality at a very deep level.

Because a good work ethic and smart genes were part of the Robinson family, both Craig and Michelle skipped the second grade. Michelle was both smart and well-behaved in school, earning her a good reputation with her teachers.

Her smarts were put to good use outside of school, as well. Her great aunt—who lived just downstairs from Michelle's family, also taught her to play the piano.

As Michelle grew older, her excellence in school earned her more attention. In 6th grade, she attended gifted classes at Bryn Maur Elementary School. This put her on the fast track to even better schooling down the road.

Attending A Magnet High School

The school system in Chicago was eager to find and reward excellence among its brightest students. Michelle Robinson was selected for such a reward when she started attending gifted classes, but that was only the beginning.

Whitney Young High School was the first magnet school in Chicago, a place for the hardest-working and brightest students to learn at an accelerated level. Michelle was invited to attend Whitney Young. While this opportunity was golden in many ways, it was also scary. How so?

First of all, this high school wasn't just down the street. It would require an hour and a half of travel from school every day. Michelle was also apprehensive about attending this faraway school filled with strange kids from across the city. How would others see her?

While Michelle continues to excel as a student, she finds other challenges in high school. For example, she'd later discuss the sexism that puzzled and sometimes infuriated her during that time. She remembers that other kids would often approach her to ask what her brother thought about a given topic instead of asking Michelle what she thought. Of course, Craig was brilliant, talented, and popular in high school, but Michelle sometimes felt overlooked.

Despite any difficulties, Michelle was determined to

do well in school. She later said that, during this time, she would take any negativity around her and use it "to fuel me, to keep me going." That attitude certainly worked because she kept herself on the honor roll throughout all four years of high school.

She also took advanced placement classes and was a proud member of the National Honor Society. At Whitney Young, she served as treasurer on the student council.

In 1981, she graduated as salutatorian of her class. After high school, Michelle had her sights set high on none other than Princeton. But would she get in?

CHAPTER 3

Princeton and Harvard

Having a sibling just ahead of you in school can be frustrating. Craig was intelligent and a good student, just like Michelle. And he was popular with both students and teachers. While Michelle may have felt she was living in her brother's shadow, she also looked up to Craig. Craig also benefited Michelle in other ways, as we'll see next.

Michelle had set her sights on Princeton. Craig was a year ahead of Michelle, and he'd entered Princeton after graduating high school. She was inspired to follow him there, aiming to enter in 1981 right after graduation.

This goal of hers wasn't universally accepted, though. Some of Michelle's teachers tried to dissuade her from applying to Princeton. They told her that she was setting her sights too high.

In other words, she needed to stay in her lane. How would she react to that discouragement? She promptly ignored it. A key theme of her life is self-knowledge, and Michelle knew what she could do and couldn't. Nevertheless, she was determined to go to Princeton, so she applied.

Later, reflecting on her life, Michelle stated that she believed her brother had a hand in helping her get accepted at Princeton. In fact, she suspected it way back then, too, because Craig was already popular with the faculty. As a result, once she was accepted, Michelle was determined to demonstrate her worth.

Of course, at the same time, she would meet new challenges while at Princeton, including a set of doubts that would cause her to question the entirety of who she was and where she was headed.

Attending Princeton

Recall the teenage Michelle Robinson, apprehensive about attending an advanced high school more than an hour from her home? The experience of going to Princeton only magnified those feelings. She'd later describe going there as completely overwhelming. And why wouldn't it be? Now she was far from the culture of south Chicago, far from her family and everything she'd known.

On top of that, Michelle would later recognize that the fact that neither of her parents had attended college meant that she didn't know what to expect when she went herself.

Princeton also made her more aware of her race than ever before. For the first time, she *felt* like a minority, and it was a strange feeling.

It wasn't just race that made Michelle feel displaced and overwhelmed. She couldn't help but notice the economic differences between her and the majority of the students there, too. "I remember being shocked," she would later say in an interview, "by college students who drove BMWs. I didn't even know parents who drove BMWs!"

The demanding workload given to college students and the racial and economic differences between Michelle and many of her classmates made her feel completely overwhelmed in her first year. Students and teachers did reach out to her, and Michelle worked hard to adjust to college life, but she often still felt like an outsider, what she called "a visitor on campus."

With racial and economic issues at the forefront of Michelle's experience at Princeton, it's no surprise that she majored in sociology and minored in African-American studies. As we'll see next, her work to help communities around her would eventually lead to a period of self-doubt, which nearly shipwrecked Michelle before she could become the leader she is today.

Senior Thesis And Self-Doubt

In 1983, Craig graduated from Princeton and became a basketball coach at Oregon University. He'd later coach basketball at Brown University. For the first time, Michelle's older brother was actually gone, and he'd left to a place that she could not follow. This was the time for her to become completely herself, free of her brother's shadow.

Not surprisingly, for anyone who knows Michelle Obama as an adult, this young Michelle spent a great deal of time giving back to the community, with a special emphasis on helping young girls and minority groups.

She got involved with the Third World Center, which is an organization that provides academic and cultural support to minority students. While running the daycare center for the TWC, she tutored older students on a variety of subjects. It was while she was tutoring at the daycare center that she challenged the way French was being taught. She claimed French classes were overly formal, focusing on rules and forms instead of conversation and culture.

In order for Michelle to graduate, she had to complete a senior sociology thesis, much like a masters or doctoral dissertation. Michelle chose the topic "Princeton-Educated Blacks and the Black

Community."

Michelle had noticed how Princeton was affecting her. She was concerned that her roots sunk deep in the African American community, especially that of south Chicago, and would conflict with the woman she was becoming. In other words, did rubbing shoulders with rich, white students and exploring higher ideals cut her off from her heritage? Did black students that graduated from Princeton (or some other elite university) still see themselves as black? Would they still be in touch with the African American communities they came from? Or did Princeton change you in an irreversible way?

In order to find answers to these meaty questions, Michelle sent 400 black Princeton alums a survey. In the survey, she asked them how comfortable they were with their race before, during, and after their time studying at Princeton. Disappointingly, only 90 people returned the survey, and the results didn't help quiet Michelle's doubts.

It seemed Michelle was "becoming" in a core sense. She could feel that who she was had changed and was still changing. But was the change something she was proud of? Would she lose touch with the communities she cared so much about?

Despite these lingering doubts, Michelle graduated *cum laude* with a Bachelor of Arts degree. Her 99-page senior thesis was completed. She left Princeton in 1985, eager to move forward to live's next great steps.

Harvard Law

The summer after she left Princeton, Michelle had some soul-searching to do. Her path was soon chosen, and she knew that she'd be able to embrace education and not lose touch with the communities she cared so much about. For this reason, Harvard Law was an ideal next step. As a lawyer, she could defend the weak and disadvantaged. She could create change in the communities that needed it the most.

When she applied to Harvard, Michelle was much more confident than before. Gone was the shy girl going to a magnet high school. Gone was the stary-eyed Princeton student that gawked at her classmate's BMWs. Now Michelle knew who she was and what her goals in life were. As one biographer wrote, "This time around, there was no doubt in her mind that she had earned her place."

Her mentor at Harvard, Charles Ogletree, commented directly on the doubts that had plagued Michelle while she was researching and writing her senior thesis at Princeton. Was she still a product of her parents and the community she'd grown up in? Or had her identity been permanently changed by the education she received at Princeton? According to Ogletree, Michelle Robinson, who stepped foot on the Harvard campus, had put all those doubts to rest. She knew who she was and was determined to be, as he put it, "both brilliant and black."

Michelle continued to aim to effect change in front of her mind while at Harvard. For example, as a student, she participated in various demonstrations, including one that advocated for hiring professors from different minority groups. During that same time, she worked for the Harvard Legal aid Bureau, assisting low-income tenants with legal cases involving their housing or rent.

In 1988, when Michelle graduated from Harvard Law with a Juris Doctor (J.D.) degree, she was mature and focused on helping others, especially those that were underprivileged or belonged to a minority. She'd later say that her education gave her opportunities beyond what she had ever imagined.

After Harvard, Michelle would go on to enter the workforce, eager to use her education in law to help others. In addition to that mission, it would be at work that Michelle would meet the man she'd later marry, as we'll talk about in the following chapter.

CHAPTER 4

Starting a Family

After graduating from Harvard, Michelle started working as a lawyer at Sidley Austin LLP. Certainly, her desire to help the underprivileged hadn't faded, but her first job was focused on marketing and intellectual property law. It wouldn't be long before she'd return to her love of helping others, as we'll see later.

In the meantime, when her mother asked her about any plans of getting married or having a family, Michelle told her she was determined to stay single and focus on her career. After all, she loved the law and the things she'd learned at Harvard. Moreover, she was determined to prove herself in the workforce, especially because she was a black woman in a world dominated by white men.

While working at Sidley and Austin, her plans changed, and that all started when a young man started working in her department—a man named Barack Obama.

Meeting Barack

Michelle would later say that when Barack was introduced to her law firm, the two of them were the only African Americans in the entire firm. That wasn't exactly true since other African Americans have come forward saying they worked at Sidley and Austin at the same time. It seems, however, that Michelle and Barack were the only black people in that particular department, so they would have felt very much a minority at work.

Whatever the case, Barack, being a summer associate, needed a mentor, and the higher-ups selected Michelle to teach him the ropes. Early on, they had a business lunch together, and there had to be at least some chemistry between them at that point. It was at a community organization meeting a short time later that Barack really caught Michelle's eye. She'd done something that is hard to do to a career-focused, intelligent woman—impress her.

And so, despite Michelle's passion for her career and determination to "stay single," she agreed to go on a first official date with Barack. They went to the movies and saw Spike Lee's film *Do the Right Thing*, a fitting name that could easily be used to describe much of Obama's life down the line.

In many ways, Michelle and Barack were opposites. For example, she was from a "conventional" background, a stable childhood in a two-parent home. On the other hand, Barack would publicly describe his childhood as "more adventurous." Yet, perhaps partially because they were so different in so many ways, their attraction grew.

This fairy-tale story wouldn't remain so happy, however, as we'll talk about next.

Love And Tragedy

The year 1991 would be a formative year for Michelle, and events during that year, many of which are tragic in nature, would significantly shape her path in life.

She and Barack were still dating, while they both also focused on their careers. Then, in March of 1991, Michelle's father, Fraser Robinson III, finally succumbed to his chronic illness, leaving Michelle's mother a widow. Michelle later said that her father had left a lifelong "hole in my heart."

This tragedy was horrible, but it was made even worse shortly after a lifelong friend named Suzanne Alele passed away suddenly from an aggressive form of cancer.

These two great losses in quick succession caused Michelle to think (or perhaps rethink) deeply about her life and where she was going. Specifically, she started to think about her contribution to society. How was she influencing the world for the good through her work? Was she creating the changes she wanted to see? Was it making an impact?

Many years later, Michelle would look back at this time and call it a turning point in her life. She'd continue to say, for a long time, that the memory of her father was still motivating her each day.

This turning point became evident in that same year of 1991. She would go on to be made Assistant to the Mayor and Assistant Commissioner of Planning and Development. These public sector positions allowed her to focus on the community and how she could help the very people she'd grown up with and around, the very schools and neighborhoods she knew from childhood, and the very streets she'd walked as a little girl. Her focus wasn't just on the law anymore, but it was brought right back to her roots and original dreams—of helping others around her.

Meanwhile, Barack shared many of her dreams and ideals, and his career took him to help others in different ways. Their relationship strengthened, and they were married on October 3, 1992.

Michelle Robinson was now Michelle Obama, and her desire to help others would continue to be a driving focus of her life. Another goal was developing in her heart, however: that of becoming a mother.

CHAPTER 5

Becoming a Mother

Now a wife, Michelle Obama continues to push forward with her career, focusing on helping the community around her stronger than ever. Shortly after their marriage, Michelle put her law license on a voluntary inactive status. Since 1993, she has not worked as a lawyer, although her education has continued to help her immensely.

In that same year, she started working as the executive director of the Chicago office of Public Allies. This non-profit organization encourages youths to give more thought about how they can help their communities by working on social issues. Basically, the organization wants children to consider career paths that lead them to non-profit groups and government organizations that help others.

Michell would go on to work for the Chicago Office of Public Allies for the next four years. During that time, she'd set a new record in fundraising for a non-profit, a record that wouldn't be broken again until 2009.

She found her work with that non-profit very rewarding. She'd later say that she'd never been happier before working with the organization. As she put it, her job was "to build public allies" by encouraging new generations of social workers and community leaders.

And yet, while Michell's career was on fire in the best way, there was another goal on the Obamas' horizon —have children and start a family.

Both Political And Parenting Ambitions

Early in her marriage, Michelle had a miscarriage. This tragic event only pushed them harder toward their dream of being parents.

The Obamas lived in a beautiful three-story house on Chicago's South Side. The brick home has gables over the windows and a quaint garden on the small front lawn. No doubt such a large house felt cold and empty without any children to fill it with love and noise.

While the desire for children still burned bright, and Michelle was actively pursuing a fulfilling career helping youths and building up communities, Barack had also set his sights on a career move that would allow him to help others.

At the time, Barack taught at the University of Chicago Law School, but the career move he had in mind would take him out of the realm of teaching. In fact, he wanted to leap from the private sector to the public sector, pursuing a future in politics.

These political ambitions bore fruit when, in 1996, he was elected to the state senate. Being a local-level politician was an easy transition. Barack didn't have to travel far to campaign or work as a state senator once he was elected.

Also, in 1996, Michelle started serving as the Associate Dean of Student Services at the University of Chicago. This work allowed her to focus on two major themes in her career: education and the community. While working at the university, she developed the school's Community Service Center.

With all these career paths taking up so much of their time, one might think that the Obamas didn't need to think about becoming parents, at least not for a while. That wasn't how Michelle saw things, and her dream was finally fulfilled when she and Barack had their first child, Malia Ann, in 1998, thanks to in vitro fertilization. Finally, their large home would be busy and filled with noise.

Motherhood And Campaigns

Along with all the joys of parenting come plenty of worries and stress. That said, Michelle loved being a mother, and she was determined to be both a great mother and to continue to help local communities through her work.

At the same time, Barack's political ambitions weren't quenched by being a state senator.

Michelle was openly unenthusiastic about Barack's political career. In fact, back in 1996, she'd said she was wary of getting involved in the campaign, mostly because she didn't like the idea of all that public scrutiny. Throughout her life, Michelle has described herself as an intensely private person, a description that doesn't mesh well with campaigning and politics.

That said, Michelle was supportive while Barack ran for the state senate, shaking hands and fundraising alongside her husband. But it certainly wasn't something she enjoyed. So when Barack came to her with the idea of running for the US house of representatives, Michelle was even more wary, and for good reason. For one thing, they now had a little girl whose privacy would also be jeopardized. On top of that, the campaign would be much larger, requiring travel across the state of Illinois. Despite these concerns, when Barack ran in 2000, Michelle was right by his side, supporting him completely.

Being supportive and being enthusiastic are two different things, however. When Barack lost the 2000 campaign for the House of Representatives, Michelle said she was glad and hoped he would just get a normal job, such as teaching at a law school once again.

Obama's future would bring new challenges, though.

Two Girls And A Senator

In 2001, Michelle had a second child, Natasha, affectionately called Sasha by both her parents and the public. With two girls at home, Michelle was more focused and determined than ever to be a good mom.

At the same time, her career continued full steam ahead. In 2002, she started working for the University of Chicago Hospitals as their director of community affairs.

Barack's career marched forward, as well. In 2004, he went campaigning once again and managed to win the 2004 election to the US Senate. With this change, it meant Barack would have to spend at least some of his time in Washington, DC. The Obamas chose to keep their girls in Chicago, though, instead of moving to the capital. They felt staying in that home, with those local schools, would be better—and more stable—for the girls.

In 2005, Michelle was named Vice President for Community and External Affairs at the University of Chicago Hospitals. Her growing career kept her busy, which was difficult because Barack had to spend a good deal of his time in DC.

Financially, Michelle was the primary breadwinner of the family in that she made nearly double what Barack made. Of course, even in a city like Chicago, Barack's yearly income as a senator of $157,000 would probably be enough to get by. However, Michelle's 273,000 dollars combined salary certainly made things easier.

Even though the Obamas were very busy, with an elementary-school daughter and another just starting school, and with Barack being gone for work quite often, they were making it work, and they were happy.

Barack, however, had a new dream, one that would really put the family to the test: he had his heart set on running for president.

CHAPTER 6

2008 Presidential Campaign

A t the start of 2007, life was already complicated for the Obama family. Michelle had a great career, and she was taking care of two young girls. She struggled to support her husband, who had to split his time between Chicago and Washington, DC. Because the family stayed in Chicago, the girls attended the University of Chicago Laboratory Schools, an award-winning private school.

Michelle was a member of the board at her daughter's school, as well. While serving as a board member, she fought for more diversity among the student body. This goal came into direct conflict with other members of the board because many wanted to reserve more slots for the family members of the faculty. This makes sense because teachers at these exclusive schools are expected to get their children into them. But Michelle wouldn't back down, saying that more children of minority groups, especially young girls, needed more opportunities for a better education. In the end, a compromise was reached, and plans were made to expand the school so there would be room for more diversity and more children of faculty.

On top of all that, Michelle and the children had to become accustomed to the "public life." After all, Barack had been involved in some sort of political venture for nearly a decade. That said, Michelle's life was about to get more complicated because running for president is far more taxing than running for a single senatorial seat.

The Early Campaign

Needless to say, since she'd already been unenthusiastic about Barack's earlier campaigns, she had strong reservations about the idea of her husband running for president. Specifically, she saw it as a possible negative effect on the girls.

Eventually, though, she negotiated a deal with Barack: he'd have to give up smoking in order for her to support him on the campaign trail. Barack gladly agreed. Even so, her supporting him didn't make him part of his staff. She repeatedly said publicly, "My job is not a senior advisor." In other words, she would not be trying to force her views or goals regarding community growth on her husband.

To keep her side of the bargain and support her husband—and to support the girls throughout the campaign—Michelle reduced her work responsibilities by about 80% in 2007. In fact, her focus on family was evident early in the campaign because she would only campaign a couple of days a week. She wanted to be home with the girls the rest of the week.

When she did speak, she was a refined and engaging speaker. She wrote her own speeches and could usually give them without using any notes. Throughout the campaign, she also appeared on Oprah Winfrey's program several times.

While Michell was determined to support the girls, her relationship with Barack was already getting strained at this point. Barack put it this way in his second book, *The Audacity of Hope: Thoughts on Reclaiming the American Dream*, "Tired and stressed, we had little time for conversation, much less for romance." While he was a Senator, however, they always tried to schedule date nights with Michelle to keep the relationship as strong as possible.

As 2007 led to 2008, and the campaign heated up, Michelle got busier. In February, she attended 38 events in just eight days. The campaign heating up also brought with it new trials and difficulties, however. Michelle would come under fire from the media and political enemies.

Trials On The Campaign Trail

The campaign in 2008 was the first time Michelle had been exposed to the national political scene. Along with all that new exposure came new trials. The media and others started to target Michelle in an effort to make Barack look bad. Michelle was up to the challenge, though.

For example, while speaking in support of her husband, she often told anecdotes about Obama's family life. In addition to talking about her family in general, she also often used her experiences as a mother as a contextual backdrop to talk about big issues like race and education, issues that have always been near and dear to her heart.

While Obama supporters loved Michelle's speaking style, many in the press zeroed in on one aspect of her way of speaking—her recurring use of sarcasm. As a result, people started calling her cold or "bitchy". Even though such descriptions were blown very much out of proportion, they were affecting her image, therefore affecting Barack's image. So Michelle worked to dial back her sarcasm during speeches and interviews.

Of course, the accusations didn't end there. a Fox News Columnist named Carl Thomas called Michelle an "Angry Black Woman," referring to her seemingly cold nature. When asked to respond to the description, Michelle said in an interview: "Barack and I have been in the public eye for many years now, and we've developed a thick skin along the way. When you're out campaigning, there will always be criticism. I just take it in stride, and at the end of the day, I know that it comes with the territory."

Thick skin or not, Michelle continued to work on her image throughout the campaign. For example, she worked on speaking softer and being more empathetic with reporters. She started to dress more casually in public, even though her sense of style was a constant focus of the media and praised by the press. They also continued to look for public forums that would be more "down to earth" than just major news outlets. For example, when she appeared on The View and was interviewed in Ladies' Home Journal, her public image became more human and well-rounded.

Overcoming these trials during the campaign, Michelle's likeability soared in the eyes of America. During the 2008 Democratic National Convention, Michelle gave the keynote address, being introduced by her older brother, Craig Robinson. In that speech, she explained that she and Barack see their family and lives as the embodiment of the American Dream. She also said that they believe that "you work hard for what you want in life, that your word is your bond, and you do what you say you're going to do, that you treat people with dignity and respect, even if you don't know them and even if you don't agree with them." Her speech was well received and got good reviews from all kinds of media personalities and commentators. In the end, Barack won the Democratic nomination and would go on to win the presidency.

Of course, political enemies continued to cause problems for the Obamas. For example, E.D. Hill, on Fox News' *America's Pulse*, made a series of claims about Barack, such as (1) he was born in Africa and therefore didn't qualify to run for president, (2) he was a Muslim, and (3) therefore was a likely terrorist. These claims culminated just after the Democratic Convention when Barack won the nomination, and he and Michelle famously fist-bumped in celebration. Hill called the fist bump a "terrorist fist jab." But that criticism was too far in many people's eyes. Hill was taken off the air shortly after, and *America's Pulse* was canceled.

Despite criticisms and outright lies, Michelle supported her husband throughout the campaign. In the end, with Michelle by his side, Barack was elected the first African American President of the United States.

CHAPTER 7

Becoming the First Lady

Moving into the White House meant big changes for the Obama family. First, Malia and Sasha had to leave Chicago and the school they'd been attending. Michelle and Barack considered Georgetown Day School, but, in the end, they chose Sidwell Friends School.

Michelle's mother also moved to the White House to help with raising the girls. Barack and Michelle sought advice from other presidential mothers, such as Laura Bush, Rosalynn Carter, and Hillary Clinton.

For Michelle, personally, big changes were on the horizon. She had to get used to being the First Lady. But what kind of First Lady would she become?

Feeling Her Way As First Lady

In her first months as First Lady, Michelle wanted to get to know Washington. First, she focused on the common people, the community, the very thing she's always been passionate about. She visited homeless shelters, soup kitchens, and local schools. This was the first time she was able to take a long, hard look at communities outside of the Chicago area, gaining an even better understanding of the ailments many American (and world) communities have in common.

She also expressed her intention of visiting all the US Cabinet-level agencies in the DC area. This was part of her effort to get acquainted with how Washington works.

While she felt her way around being the First Lady, Michelle was still applauded for her sense of style. From the very beginning, the media often focused on Michelle's outfits, even to the point of being criticized for not giving enough attention to the messages Michelle was trying to communicate at times.

Michelle was on the cover of the march 2009 issue of Vogue, making her the second-ever First Lady to be on the cover.

Meanwhile, she continued to speak on various public occasions. For example, she promoted bills that supported her husband's policy priorities. While her involvement in politics, though slight, was praised by some, others felt she was becoming too involved. After all, as one reporter put it, "Nobody voted for Michelle Obama." Even so, she continued to find her way as First Lady, hosting a White House reception for women's rights advocates, this being around the same time that the Lilly Ledbetter Fair Pay Act of 2009 was enacted.

In April of 2009, Michelle traveled to the UK, making this her first trip abroad as First Lady. At Buckingham Palace, she met Queen Elizabeth II. They hugged before attending an event with world leaders, and that hug sparked a good deal of controversy because Michelle had acted out of protocol. The Queen didn't seem to mind, though. On that same trip, she toured a cancer ward with Sarah Brown, the wife of Prime Minister Gordon Brown. The media called this trip Michell's demonstration of "star power."

In May of 2009, she gave the commencement speech at the graduating ceremony in US Merced, which is in California. The speech was well received, and people later called it "straightforward and relatable." The San Francisco Chronicle noted the chemistry between Michelle and the students. In that same year of 2009, Michelle was named Barbara Walter's "Most Fascinating Person of the Year."

Michelle was getting used to being First Lady, but it would be the following year that she'd really come into her own at the White House.

Standing Up For Important Issues

Michelle's second year as First Lady was when she essentially "became" the First Lady she is remembered as now. The year 2010 was about much more than star power or good chemistry between her and her audience. Gone were the days she was trying to get used to Washington. Michelle was ready to become the role model she was destined to be.

This bolder and more active Michelle started to focus on issues she believed in, such as children's health, stronger communities, more opportunities for girls and people of minorities, and better education, especially for young women.

For example, in January of 2010, Michelle took the lead in an initiative called "let's Move!" which was focused on trying to reverse the trend of childhood obesity. "Let's Move!" was officially announced in February, and Barack also created a Task Force on Childhood Obesity. Several military generals even backed this initiative because obesity was a growing problem among new recruits across all branches of the military.

For Michelle, "Let's Move!" was not just another bland political initiative. Instead, she wanted her fight against child obesity to be part of her legacy. "I want to leave something behind that we can say,

'Because of this time this person spent here, this thing has changed,'" she famously said. "My hope is that that's going to in the area of Childhood Obesity."

In April of 2010, Michelle traveled on her own to Mexico. This was her first time traveling abroad as First Lady without Barack also traveling to the same country. In Mexico, she spoke to students, encouraging them to take responsibility for their own futures. She pointed out that underprivileged children can set their sights high. "Potential can be found in some of the most unlikely places," she said. She used herself and her husband as examples of this.

As 2010 progressed, Michelle was seen as a universal role model, especially for young girls. Her sense of style was also seen as a good example. She was regularly compared to Jacqueline Kennedy. She wore clothes designed by world-renowned fashion artists, but she also wore less-expensive brands, like J. Crew and Target. It was said that others so meticulously imitated her style that her patronage of a brand could mean a $14 million boost to the company.

All this popularity meant that Michelle was in high demand to help with the midterm elections. Plenty of Democrat candidates begged her to come and speak on their behalf. Early in 2010, Michelle had said she wasn't sure if she'd help anyone's campaign. But she later changed her mind, visiting seven states in two weeks in October. She refused to get involved in deep political discussion while campaigning, however. In the end, it appears her support didn't move the needle significantly for those elections.

However, this bolder and more active First Lady continued to travel and speak about issues that mattered to her. For example, In June of 2011, she went on a tour of Africa to Johannesburg, Cape Town, and Botswana. She supported local community programs and worked to advance her husband's foreign policy.

Back in the 2008 presidential campaign, Michelle often spoke of LGBT rights. She would often mention how Barack had supported the Illinois Human Rights Act and the Illinois Gender Violence Act. Barack had also supported the Employment Non-Discrimination Act. Up to this point, however, they had never officially come out in favor of same-sex marriages.

In September of 2011, Don't Ask Don't Tell was repealed, and Michelle made a point of including openly gay service members in her national military families initiative.

As of the middle of 2011, talk of Obama's re-election was already warming up, and that meant a new roller-coaster ride for Michelle and her family, as we'll see next.

Obama's Re-Election Campaign

Up to this point, Michelle had been avoiding talking about her husband's presidential re-election. By the end of 2011, however, she had grown so much as a role model and public figure that her approval rating was staying steady at over 60%. She was even being called "the most popular political figure in America" by political pundits.

During the re-election campaign, Barack wasn't doing as well against Romney as expected. This was partly because he was being called cold and detached by the media. For example, he often looked down when addressing Romney in their debates. With Obama and Romney neck and neck, both claiming about 47% of the female vote, it was time for Michelle to jump in to support her husband.

She worked to humanize her husband by telling personal stories about him. For example, at the 2012 Democratic National Convention, she said, "Barack knows the American Dream because he's lived it. And he wants everyone in this country to have that same opportunity, no matter where we are, or where we're from, or what we look like, or who we love."

Ann Romney was doing the same kind of thing for her husband, but Michelle's popularity certainly gave her an advantage when it came to humanizing and supporting her husband. In the end, though, as

Michelle Cottle of Newsweek pointed out, "Nobody votes for the First Lady."

Barack really stepped up in the end, squeezing out a win and a second term as president.

2012—A Busy Year

Aside from the intense campaign trail, Michelle had a busy year in 2012. She was continually growing as First Lady and becoming more passionate about the issues she was standing behind.

The Obamas worked hard to support military families and spouses. They spent time listening to the stories of veterans—even when their time could have been spent more wisely from a campaign perspective. Michelle was often moved to tears when hearing these stories. In April of 2012, the Obamas were awarded the Jerald Memorial Founders' Award by the National Coalition for Homeless Veterans. This is a high honor, in fact, the highest honor that can be given to an advocate for homeless veterans.

In addition, "Let's Move!" was gaining momentum. While previous First Ladies had ordered the White House kitchen to use organic foods in preparing their meals, Michelle went a step further by planting an organic garden on the grounds of the White House. This was the first White House garden since the days of Eleanor Roosevelt. Michelle also had bee hives added to the South Lawn to tend to flowering plants in the region and provide honey.

In 2012, Michelle published a book entitled *American Grown: The Story of the White House Kitchen Garden and Gardens Across America*, which helps to promote healthy eating and gardening.

On May 9, 2012, the Obamas officially came out in favor of same-sex marriages. Michelle said, "This is an important issue for millions of Americans, and for Barack and me, it really comes down to the values of fairness and equality we want to pass down to our girls... discriminating against same-sex couples just isn't right."

Completing their first term as President and First Lady of the United States of America was no small feat for Michelle and her family. The next four years would allow Michelle to continue to lead and speak on matters she cared about. It would also be when her possible political ambitions became a major question on the minds of members of the media and the public in general. We'll see all this and more in the chapter that follows.

CHAPTER 8

A Second Term

I n August of 2013, Michelle attended an event at the Lincoln Memorial—the 50th-anniversary ceremony for the march on Washington. This historic event meant a lot to Black Americans, but the press decided to spend much of their time and energy focusing on what Michelle wore: a black sleeveless dress with red flowers. The dress was designed by Tracy Reese, who later told the press, "I'm honored that she would choose to wear one of our designs during the celebration of such a deeply significant historical moment."

The press would eventually come under fire for focusing so much on Michelle's fashion and less on the issues to which she was trying to give voice to. But that wouldn't be before political enemies used this focus to criticize Michelle herself. For example, Michelle Cottle put out a Politico article, called her a "feminist nightmare" because she wasn't doing more to push for women's issues. Cottle noted the focus on Michelle's trendy styles and on things like gardening and healthy eating, saying, "She's essentially becoming the English lady of the manor."

Cottle's criticisms were met with backlash, however. Michelle's supporters noted that Michelle wasn't just "talking about healthy eating"; she was leading the charge against childhood obesity by aggressively promoting good eating habits. Obesity, it turns out, continues to be a major health crisis in the US.

This controversy led the media to realize they needed to focus more on Michelle's message and less on her dress.

In March of 2014, she traveled to China with her daughters and mother. There, they met Peng Liyuan, the wife of President Xi Jinping. Together, they toured several cultural sights and schools. Michelle's purpose in this trip, as stated by her, was to "show that the relationship between the US and China is not just between leaders. It's a relationship between peoples."

Non-Stop Traveling

The second half of this second term meant a great deal of traveling for Michelle, where she was able to display even more of that well-earned "star power."

In January of 2015, she traveled to Saudi Arabia with Barack. This was just after King Abdullah died, and they met with King Salman. Michelle would once again be criticized for not following protocol, this time because she didn't cover her head in the king's presence. Salman did not greet or acknowledge her in any way, although it is difficult to know if this is because she is a woman or because her head was not covered. Others saw this as Michelle standing up for women's rights and showing a great deal of courage. Plus, as a foreigner, it is not automatically expected that she follow the same customs as the women of Saudi Arabia.

In March of that year, the entire Obama family went to Selma, Alabama to commemorate the 50th anniversary of the Selma-to-Montgomery marches. They even crossed the Edmund Pettus Bridge alongside some of the still-living original marchers.

In June, the entire family, including Michelle's mother, went on a weeklong trip to London and three Italian cities. There, they met with British Prime Minister David Cameron and Prince Harry. On this trip, Michelle spoke about international education for adolescent girls, a topic she is very passionate about.

A few months later, in October, Michelle joined forces again with Prince Harry. She, the prince, and Jill Biden visited a military base at Fort Belvoir, Virginia. This was part of Prince Harry's initiative to raise awareness of programs supporting injured service members.

In November, Michelle traveled once again to the Middle East, this time to Qatar. This was to discuss her initiative to advance international education opportunities for young women. She spoke at the World Innovation Summit for Education, talking about her "Let Girls Learn" initiative. She'd planned to go to Amman, Jordan to tour a school there, but the weather conditions in the area didn't allow for that to happen.

The following month, in December, the Obamas went to San Bernardino, California to support the community after a terrorist attack.

With all of this travel and speaking, and the "star power" Michelle had summoned, many people wondered: Would Michelle Obama plan to run for president?

Michelle Obama For President?

As early as the spring of 2015, people started asking if Michelle planned to run for president after her husband's second term. In fact, around that time, some polls put her as the favorite above both Bernie Sanders and Hillary Clinton for the Democratic nomination.

In 2016, the Obamas continued to travel, going to

Cuba to aid in Cuban-US relations. It was on this trip that Michelle made it clear to the press that she didn't intend to run.

Barack was pressed about the issue in a town hall meeting, as well. He said, "There are three things that are certain in life: death, taxes, and Michelle is not running for president. That I can tell you."

A few months later, in March of 2016, Michelle was in Austin when she told the press that she'd never run. Instead, she'd decided to "impact as many people as possible in an unbiased way."

After making this clear, Michelle opened the way for Hillary Clinton to run in the 2016 election.

Michelle was happy to support Hillary Clinton during that campaign, speaking on her behalf several times. After Clinton got the Democratic nomination, Michelle continued to travel and speak in her support. But, of course, in the end, Donald Trump won the election, replacing Barack Obama and promising to do his best to undo everything Obama had done while in office.

As we'll see next, however, Barack Obama—and Michelle, as well—had left behind a legacy that couldn't be easily erased.

CONCLUSION

After eight years in the White House, the Obamas left a strong legacy behind. But, more than that, they also both continued to speak out on the issues that they cared about most.

For example, in May of 2017, Michelle spoke at the Partnership for a Healthier American conference. There, she rebuked Trump yet again, this time because his administration was delaying a federal requirement to increase the nutritional value of school lunches.

In June, she attended the WWDC in Silicon Valley, in which she talked about another passion project of hers—diversity. She talked about how tech companies needed to diversify their ranks.

In July of 2017, she was honored by Eunice Shriver at the ESPY Awards. In September, she spoke at a tech conference in Utah, once again hitting on the topic of diversity. She also called Trump's White

House a "fearful White House." That same month, she appeared in a video at the Global Citizen Festival pushing for education for young girls.

Michelle continued to be a big-ticket speaker for many conferences and events, just like Barack has been since leaving Washington. Michelle often speaks about diversity, education for women, and how there needs to be more women in politics.

Becoming

Michelle's memoir, *Becoming* was published in November of 2018 and sold over 11 million copies in its first 30 days.

In 2020, a Netflix documentary of the same name, which shows Michelle on the book tour for her memoir, was released in 2020. In her epilogue for the book, she reiterates her lack of desire to run for president, saying, "I have no intention of running for office, ever. Politics can be a means for positive change, but this area is just not for me."

Since then, Michelle released the Michelle Obama Podcast, which continues to occasionally put out new episodes, even though it's mostly used to promote other podcast series or shows that she or Barack have appeared on.

In a larger sense, however, *Becoming* is much more than the name of a book or documentary. It's a central theme of her life. She's transitioned from independent career woman to wife and mother and community leader to fashion trendsetter and role model to the kind of person many would love to see run for president.

Michelle Robinson started life with a rich background, but she has spent her whole life becoming something else. And she pushes others around her to become... to grow in amazing ways.

We've also seen in her life to date how she has managed to balance incredible responsibilities. We've seen her embrace education for herself and push for a better education for girls and others around the world.

We also see in Michelle someone that knows herself and who is comfortable with who she is. And because of this, she is not easily swayed to becoming something she is not. Instead, she marches straight on, doing the same thing she's always done: work to build better communities and give others around her the opportunity to become the very best versions of themselves.

Made in United States
Orlando, FL
24 August 2024

50710645R00038